Songs to My Beloved
*Passionate Prayers to
the Lover of My Soul*

Songs to My Beloved
Passionate Prayers to the Lover of My Soul

Heather Van Dam

© 2004
Express Media Publishers

© 2004 by Heather Van Dam

All Scripture quotations, unless otherwise indicated, are taken from the HOLY BIBLE, NEW INTERNATIONAL VERSION®, copyright© 1973. 1978, 1984 by International Bible Society. Used by permission of Zondervan Publishing House. All rights reserved. The "NIV" and "New International Version" trademarks are registered in the United States Patent and Trademark Office by International Bible Society. Use of either trademark requires the permission of International Bible Society.

Scripture quotations marked KJV are taken from the King James Version of the Bible.

All quotes and material set without a source are written by Heather Van Dam.

Cover photo by Heather Van Dam © 2004
Materials in this book are protected by copyright law, and may not be reprinted without the express permission of the author. She welcomes your comments and requests.
hvandam@frontiernet.net

With a deeply grateful heart, I
thank my Beloved for giving me
a family legacy of prayer warriors,
grandparents on both sides –
Anna and Howard,
Marie and Floyd,
who gave me my father and mother.
It deeply affected me to see
Mom slip away to her room to
intercede when one of us was in need.
She was in her room a lot.
Early in the mornings I could
always find my father
kneeling in prayer, or prostrate
on his face before God.

To Barbara and John –
Mama and   Daddy - thank you
for covering us in Love.
It saved my brother, sister and me.

Your prayers availed much.
They still do.

Guidelines and a challenge:

Why didn't you capitalize the pronouns referring to Beloved in your poetry?

Though it may seem odd to see "him" and "his" in lower case letters, I followed the format of Scripture in doing this, not because I don't have the highest respect for my Beloved, but because I wanted the text of poetry to flow without impediment and to read like poetry which would be written to a lover. God is The Lover of my soul and I always think of him in capitals.

How do you use capital letters and italics?

When I address the Lover of my soul it is always as Beloved capital B. When there is reference to a believer, it will be lower case b - beloved. I use *italics* when the Beloved speaks – through his Word or as he conveys himself in a personal way to the individual – logos and rhema.

Are you up for a new adventure?

A simple method of study, which opened the understanding of Scripture to me on a whole new level, was the use of color coding. I took a new Bible and highlighted all the verses about God's faithfulness and man's perseverance in blue, God directly answering prayer in pink. Looking at the results brought incredible revelation about prayer. Except for the verses from Song of Songs, others given here are taken from "the pink." God has always answered his people, and still does! Use other colors for your own study. I used these: green for verses where God defends his children and spiritual warfare, purple for grace, yellow for "keys to the faith", and I underline verses in red that speak of salvation. You can add symbols – stars by verses about hope or glory, upward spirals next to verses on joy, etc. I can open my Bible and see at a glance the topics I'm researching, and more - these show spiritual patterns and principles: try this and then look at all the blue and pink in the Gospels and book of Acts! You may not want to lay your Bible down. Ask God for new revelation. He wants you to know him better.

Comments about prayer:

"I ask. Nothing happens. Why bother?"

"I don't know about you, but God answers my prayers!"

"I know the 'Our Father'."

"There is nothing like the peace that comes from communing with the Lord."

"I love to talk with God. I ask and He answers. I'm spoiled, now that I've become used to hearing from Him. I want Him all the time."

"If God's gonna' do what He wants anyway, then why try to influence Him?"

"Prayer changes things."

"I love talking to and hearing from my Lover."

The #1, all-time most popular prayer:

" Help!"

Introduction

Since 9/11 there has come a fresh breath from God that has left His people gasping for the sheer wonder of it. How did this happen? Very simply, people prayed. Millions of people were galvanized by the terrorist attacks on the World Trade Towers in New York City and on the Pentagon in Washington to pray more fervently than ever before for the condition of this world. Many of us knew and lost people in those attacks. As believers, we found ourselves seriously considering the ones who are facing eternity without the Savior and have become moved to tears over it. Intercessors around the world have gone deeper into intercessory prayer. We have been awakened at all hours of the night and beckoned throughout the day by the Spirit of God, to stand in the gap for people who need prayer.

For me, this deepening into Jesus escalated five years ago when God pulled me from the middle of a whirlwind career in education with a diagnosis of Lupus – a chronic autoimmune disease that, for unknown reasons, causes the immune system to attack the body's own healthy tissue and organs. I began to have as many as 20 seizures a month as the disease attacked my central nervous system, thyroid and endocrine system. The list of symptoms was long, but the bottom line was that I was debilitated and bed-ridden for almost two years before I was able to spend an hour or two a day up. All my work and ministry - what I had been doing in school, at church, my professional and social lives – all came to a screeching halt. Life as I knew it, was over.

I am a little better now – but there is nothing like having only two or three hours a day to be up and around to help you choose what is most important. I can only say "Praise God!" for his plans for my liberation. I know that we mortals do not have the foresight to see the wisdom in the ways God sometimes chooses to work.

How could I have known that my Abba would use a debilitating disease as a portal to a whole new life of freedom? He designed and carried out a profound emotional and spiritual healing for me, one I would not have had, had the rug not been pulled out from under me; had I not come to the absolute end of myself; had I not been desperate. These years of quiet and alone time with him led to my being able to really learn to know his heart and recognize his voice. This then led me to begin a healing prayer and drama ministry to help the wounded find a complete recovery. And don't kid yourself, every one of us has our wounds.

These last five years have brought so many surprises! Even loving the Lord as much as I have in my lifetime did not prepare me for discovering that I could fall passionately in love with him and to learn to know him as Lover.

> " It's happened
> and no help for it.
> I'm head over heels
> in love with you,
> Beloved."

I cannot seem to get enough of him. As when you try to sit on a rubber ball in a swimming pool, my thoughts, when they meander to any other these days, simply bound out of the water to Jesus. And what he has shown me is that when we welcome him with an open heart, he will not only pour himself out into our spirits, but will do so on ever-increasing levels every day. We can always have more! And when we become so filled with him that we do not see how we can possibly hold another revelation of love, we have only to ask and he will "Enlarge the place of your tent, stretch your tent curtains wide…lengthen your cords, strengthen your stakes. " (Isaiah 54:2 NIV) as many times as we want. In other words, Jehovah will go as far with us in revealing himself in all his glory, as we are willing to have him go. We can have more than dreams of loving and being loved intimately by God – our Beloved. It is what He wants! It is what he designed us for. He is just waiting to be given permission to flood us with a superabundant life through himself! This degree of capacious love is ours for the asking.

Think of a person you highly admire and respect... It is one thing to imagine this person at your home, yet quite another to see him or her actually holding hands around your dinner table, blessing the food and then discussing your most heartfelt issues.

And that is nothing! We can have in-depth conversations with the Lord, and during times of unimagined intimacy, not only touch his face, but feel him loving us in whatever way we most need to be loved. We can become aware that our very cells are vibrating with the fullness of his presence; that he has not only heard us, but is here with us, responding from within. The lover of our souls kisses us in ways that alter us forever. My Lover and I share spiritual ecstasy.

I have never known there could be such deep relationship with the Lord of Lords. You know that he loves you and that you love him. But did you suspect that you could be in love with each other? That he is eager to be with you – has butterflies of excitement looking forward to alone times? He can give you butterflies of excitement just thinking about Him.

It's possible. It's happened! I never knew that when he said, "I will never leave you or forsake you" that I could feel his actual presence all the time; that when I began to worship him, he would take that worship and transport me to the highest planes;

that he could perform through me, miracles that are clearly beyond my capabilities of expression, so that people can only see them and glorify my Father in heaven.

I have received my heart's desires from the Lover of my soul! And so can you. If you have been longing for a deeper relationship, more intimacy and overcoming power, then go to God and ask him to teach you to hear his voice. You can know his Voice: it is different from your own thoughts and is different from the voice of the Accuser. It is not the voice of the world. His Voice is unmistakable. And as you practice listening for him and running to do his bidding you will find a new life – one that is free. To do God's will is the most joyful and fulfilling habit you can have. You will be spoiled as you compare mere human-motivated living to the kind you find in him.

Ultimately, my fantasy is to so learn the heart and thoughts of God, that I cannot separate them from my own. I want to go from "In all thy ways acknowledge him and he shall direct they paths" (Proverbs 3:6 KJV) to
"Delight yourself in the Lord, and he shall give thee the desires of your heart." (Psalm 37:4 KJV)

On the following pages you will find passionate outpourings to my Beloved, actual cries from the depth of a heart which, maybe like yours, has had the word of Christ dwelling richly within it for decades. Maybe you are new to the faith and have just put your trust and life in his hands. Praise God! You are in for glory if you are seeking to know him fully now. And maybe you consider yourself to be a seeker – one who has not yet settled on how you see God. I'm so glad you're here. If you read these pages as a seeker, I believe that God will meet you here and reveal himself to you.

"You will seek me and find me. When you seek me with all your heart." Jeremiah 29:13

I know this: God was waiting for me to be ready for him. He is waiting for you too. Our Beloved is patiently waiting for us to come and ask to see Him as he is. How it must please him when we determine to abandon stereotypes of who we thought he was in order to discover who he really is. I believe that he is delighted to come to us as a "fresh breath" once we understand that he probably will not come to us this time the same way he came the last time; that though his Word and character never change, the way he problem-solves and teaches is constantly new and innovative.

So here is a challenge for you: ask God to demonstrate that "The effectual, fervent prayer of a righteous person avails much – [actually works!]" Ask him to turn your thinking upside down, to help you think more like he does. Permit him room to work in you the way he wishes he could if he had your permission and cooperation. And then, look out! Because when heaven and earth meet through the Holy Spirit in you, things will be different – they will be turned upside down. And isn't it about time for this to happen? Aren't you sick of the weak ways in which we wish for something to be different ; to be better, but it doesn't get beyond talk?

You will become a transformed person through the renewing of your mind if you are ready to stop talking about wanting more and willing to go get it. Let's ask him to come get us!

These are not the writings spilling from an active imagination, but the record of my actual experience of falling in love with Jesus Christ.

This little book is the journaling of his interactions with his beloved – me!

It is the outpouring of my soul to my Beloved.

My darling is here with me.

I am my Beloved's and he is mine.

This book is dedicated to my Lover.
I worship you with my life, Beloved.

(from the apostle Paul):

*I pray that out of his glorious riches he may strengthen you with power through his Spirit in your inner being, so that Christ may dwell in your hearts through faith. And I pray that you, being rooted and established in love, may have power, together with all the saints, to grasp how wide and long and high and deep is the love of Christ, and to know this love that surpasses knowledge – that you may be filled to the measure of all the fullness of God. Now unto him who is able to do **immeasurably more** than all we ask or imagine, according to his power that is at work within us, to him be glory...!*
Ephesians 3:16-20

"immeasurably more" has also been translated as "exceedingly abundantly"("above what we ask or think") and is the combination of two Greek words ὑπέρ – huper (hoop-er') meaning beyond, more than, exceeding, and the word περισσος - perissŏs (per-is-sos'). The word fully means "exceedingly abundant: superabundant in quantity, superior in quality. (*Strong's Concordance – Greek dictionary section, pp.57, 74*) This is what we have with our Beloved , if we want it.

A prayer to become his child:

Dear God,
    I know I have sinned – everyone has. And so I come to you now to ask you to remove that sin. By your dying on the cross for me, I know that you take my sin away. I believe that you did die for me, and I receive you as my Savior right now. Show me how to live a new life in you. Thank you that I am yours and will live with you in heaven when this life is through. In Jesus' Name.

_____ is now a Christian,
     (your name)
a believer in Christ with a new life, on this date:

_____

Welcome to the family, beloved.

Here is a prayer of dedication if you wish to use it.

Beloved,
 I release to you, and bind my heart, soul, body and mind to you – the only one who is the perfect Father. Come and teach me who you are. Give me a heart and mind like yours. I give you permission to turn my thinking upside down. Sensitize my heart to sin and teach me about repentance. Show me how to have the kind of life you want to give me. I would like to be more attracted to you – to be able to want to give you all of me to use in any way you wish. Bring me to the place where I do want to. I believe. Help my unbelief. Teach me, Father, how to love.

In Jesus' Name, amen.

My lover spoke and said to me,
'Arise, my darling,
my beautiful one,
and come with me.
See! The winter is past;
the rains are over and gone.
flowers appear on the earth;
The season of singing has come,
the cooing of doves
is heard in our land.
The fig tree forms its early fruit;
the blossoming vines spread
their fragrance.
Arise, come, my darling;
my beautiful one,
come with me.'

Song of Songs 2: 10—13

It's happened,
    and no help for it.
I'm head over heels
    in love with you
        Beloved.

Beloved,
> All these years
>> I've wanted you like this…
> and now you are here.

> The reality is so far
>> beyond the wanting.

Sweetheart!
   Tucked away in my memory treasure box
   are moments of exquisite beauty –
   the ones that define my existence:
   not only the rising Phoenix times,
      but the kiss of sunshine
         at the edge of a shadow,
      a single dew drop,
      a small, water-smoothed stone.
   I treasure the reminders of you –
    who you are as you love.
   The precious ones – people in our lives
      in their every mood,
   paint the landscape of my love life.
   And all these earthly reminders,
      beauty-breathing things,
      are the touch-stones, reminders
   that I am to squander your heart here,
         Beloved.

Beloved,
    If we become
    what we love,
    then let my kisses
    cover you
    with adoration.
    My lips
    pay homage
    to the glory
        of your beauty.

Beloved,
    You are my intoxicant,
    the exhilaration of living.
    Never,
        never
          do I want you to be
          out of my conscious mind.
   Hear me now
        in the fervency of my request:
        give me more of you,
        heart's desire.
  I already have you,
        so know that what I am asking
        is for a consummate oneness,
          a single-mindedness,
        the rhapsody of you
          wrapped in the
        one-ness of us.

As I was with Moses,
so I will be with you;
I will never leave you
or forsake you.

Joshua 1:5

Beloved,

    Longing compels me
        toward a pure
        simpatico
        with you,
    so carefully listening,
    so finely attuned,
        that I become
    an exemplar of
        just how fine
        rapport
        can be
        between lovers.

I dream about you, you know.
    Yes, Beloved, it's true.
    We are walking along the beach
        feeling no need for talk.
    Our eyes say it all.
    We smile easily.
    I look at your hands
        as you let your arms
        relax at your sides,
        an easy swing to them.
    They are hands that have known work –
        man's work:
        your fingernails are a bit ragged,
        and there is some dirt under your nails.
    They are the most beautiful hands
        I have ever seen.
        I hold one to my lips
        and kiss it.

One of your most endearing qualities
    is your laugh.
I would do anything to hear it, Beloved.
You always bless me with it,
    the best kind – unexpected, free,
    when I least expect it,
    or most need it.
Remember the time we met at the kitchen table?
It was our traditional January meeting
    where you tell me our new word
      for the year – the one you want me
    to grow into, like "equanimity".
Very seriously I asked,
    "What are my instructions?"
And you answered,
    "You're such a pip."
We both exploded with laughter.
    PIP – "Prepared in Prayer".
I just had to lay my head on my Bible
    and go with it.

How do I love thee?
    Let me count the ways…
    There's the way you let me rant and rave
        without a word of comment,
            just so I can get it off my chest.
    The way you forgive me
        when I confess what I've done,
            every single time.
    And if that wasn't enough,
        when I feel bad
        and maybe bring it up again,
    there's that way you have
        of looking puzzled and saying,
    "What are you talking about?"
        because it's gone from your memory.
    (Next year for Christmas, maybe you could
    give me *that* gift.)
    Did I understand correctly that there are
    times when your beloved can bless you?
        Is it true that faith amazes you?

Then Beloved, let me astound you
    with mine.
        I am in love with you,
        and I want you to be
        absolutely blown away
        by how much I trust you.
Help me out here.
        I believe.
        (Help my unbelief!)
If I am going to amaze you,
    even that
        has to come from you

O people of Zion, who live in Jerusalem,
you will weep no more.
How gracious he will be when you
*cry for help!
As soon as he hears, he will answer you.
Although the Lord gives you
the bread of adversity
and the water of affliction,
your teachers will be hidden no more;
with your own eyes you will see them.
Whether you turn to the right
or to the left,
your ears will hear a voice behind you saying,
'This is the way; walk in it.'
Isaiah 30:19-21

*The Hebrew word for "cry" is qârâ' (kaw-raw') and means "to call out to". It is used throughout the Old Testament, and is how believers were first known – as those who cried out to God.

oh
Beloved…
it
is
all
gone…
every
thing
i
once
held
dear –

stripped
away –

torn…

i'm
shivering
like
a
leaf
in
the
wind

save me

9/11 2001

Precious

Jesus,

I

cannot

think.

but

I

know…

Precious

Jesus…

Beloved.

(in the weeks following 9/11 as more bodies were identified.)

Here you are, Beloved,
    I see you around me,
    all around, everywhere…
There you are
    in a scale of laughter from,
    yes,
    a sleeping child,
        dreaming delights.
You moved me,
    unmoored me from my sadness
        through a firefighter's sacrifice,
        a pastor's warmth,
        a Christmas day snowfall,
        a spouse's spontaneous caress.
I soak in all the sights,
    sounds,
    touches,
    scents of you.
I need all your kisses.
(9/11/2002 1 year anniversary)

To the Lord I cry aloud
*   and he answers me from his holy hill.*
*   Psalm 3:4*

You hear, O Lord, the desire of the afflicted;
*   you encourage them,*
and you listen to their cry, defending the
*   fatherless and the oppressed,*
in order that man, who is of the earth,
*   may terrify no more.*

*   Psalm 10: 17-18*

Beloved,
    break me open
    and let the scent of spices
    fill the room.
You showed me how;
you went first
    with your Complete Brokenness;
Now I offer you mine.
Receive it
    as a wedding gift to my Beloved;
to the one who covers me
    with the effervescent myrrh of his kisses.

I will praise the Lord, who counsels me;
even at night my heart instructs me.
Psalm 16:7

I call on you, O God, for you will answer me;
give ear to me and hear my prayer.
Show the wonder of your great love,
you who save by your right hand
those who take refuge in you
from their foes.
Psalm 17: 6-7

Oh my Beloved,
    How my heart surges
        at the thought of you.
    I close my eyes,
        lower my head,
        and bend my knees.
    Here comes the stretching out of my arms
        in front of me.
    I will open my eyes;
        here I stand, poised and ready.
    After a brief pause …
        I throw myself forward,
            swan diving
        into the pool
            of your merciful healing.

Darling,
        when I ebb,
you flow;
        when I wane,
you wax;
        when I cool,
Your flame remains steady.
Your passion
        and your faithfulness
continually pull me up,
        put me back
and set me straight.

One more time, Beloved,
        one more time.

Beloved,
    How do you do it?
    How do you go to the core
        of the pain and sear the wound
        so that it closes
        and gives me no more trouble?
    How do you take me to the memory
        that has caused the torture,
        show me how you see it,
    and replace it with the new picture –
        the one that erases the old,
        and through forgiveness
        ushers in the new?
    How do you do it?
        No matter.
        Will you do it once again?

Hear my voice when I call, O Lord,
be merciful to me
and answer me.

Psalm 26:7

The Lord confides in those
who fear [have reverential trust in] him.
He makes his covenant
known to them.

Psalm 25:14

Dearest,
    It has happened.
    It has really happened:
    you have healed me –
    fully removed the sting of past hurts.
    You have erased the emotional,
        the spiritual,
        the psychological scars.
    What was for so long a divided person –
        two people in here –
           the desperate
           and the joyful,
    is now one – the jubilant!
    All the time once spent in anguish,
    is now time open to the Divine.
    I am whole and full of you;
    full, and spilling over
    with your wonderful, surging Spirit.

Beloved,
> Let's sing!
> *We are one, for you live*
> *In the temple that is me.*
> *My Beloved one's here*
> *For the world to see.*
> *As I bask in the love*
> *Who's my heart's desire,*
> *I am filled with his holy fire!*

The chorus once again!
> *As I bask in the love*
> *Who's my heart's desire,*
> *I am filled with his holy fire!*

Beloved,
    I am lovesick –
    yes, walking into furniture,
        and writing love poems;
        thoroughly preoccupied with you,
        yet as clearheaded as I've ever been.
    You have taken me over with love.
        What the poets write is true,
        and I am "counting the ways…"
        You are my crimson tide.
    It won't work as a playacting part;
    this kind of love cannot be
        orchestrated into existence
        or brought about by wishful thinking.
    You brought it to me.
    I sought the idea of love,
        but you found me with the real thing.
    You came with this great gift
        and now the old me is finished;
        the new creature changed forever
        by the reality of you.

On the breath of passion,
        love reaches out
                to touch a diverse world.
    This kind of love
        fervently seeks others.
            It will not be stilled.
No,
        love will not be stilled
            when the time is short.

    Beloved,
        set free the passion.

Was there ever such an adventure,
    as life with you, Beloved?
If I had known
    what it would be like
        to give myself over
        to Love,
I would have done it from the start.
    Thank you for not giving up on me,
    for seeing ahead to what would be.

You have held me in your heart,
        anticipating this time,
        waiting for me to realize
        how much I have needed you,
        and to discover for myself
        how powerful that love would be.

... kiss me

with the kisses of [your] mouth,

for your love

is more delightful than wine.

Song of Songs 1:2

Beloved,
    I am heavy lidded
        with love for you.
    I try to eat
        but can only
            smile;
    there are just too many
        thoughts of you.

You, Beloved, are
> the place where
> my mind resides,
> and my heart
> calls home.

A true release
> can only occur
> where there is
>> a full reception.

The flow between
> two hearts
>> where all is given,
>> all received,
> helps define the
>> love relationship
>> between us.

Beloved,
> you are my full expression.

Beloved,
    Set my tempo today.
    Let your heart be
        the metronome
        of my equanimity.

    Godspeed.

My sheep listen to my voice;
I know them,
and they follow me.

John 10:27

Beloved,
    You have emancipated me
    with an anointed throat
        touched by the oil of gladness.
    Through it pours
        your praises
        and your laughter;
    these tumble out in
        unbridled
        outright
        all-out
        across-the-board
        plumb
delight.

Darling,
    Let me sky write your name.
    I want to hire a Cessna,
        no, a Concord
    and have it trail a banner
        that says,
  "RECEIVE THE GIFT OF LOVE FROM
  THE ONE WHO INVENTED IT!"
Then I would pray
    that every human being
    would see it,
        understand,
    want it,
        believe.

Here I am,
> grown quiet and reflective,
> gentled by the nearness
> and the absolute wonder
> of you.

Then, I find us dancing,
> as lilting scales of laughter
>> effervesce
> like a natural hot spring,
> or a solar flare off the sun.

I've become a pulsar,
> and it's all your fault,

Beloved.

All your fault.

How beautiful you are,
my darling!
Oh, how beautiful!

Song of Songs 1:15

Beloved, darling,
    Let's have breakfast
        out on the porch.
    I really need the
        early morning breezes
        and you.
    I need you.
    What shall we eat this morning?
    I'm having eggs, toast, melon
        and a decaf.
    What are you having?
    A heap of freshly browned fish,
    black bread with some olive oil,
        and melon.
    Decaf? Tea?
        A tall glass of cool water.
    It's perfectly you – treating yourself.
        You are my treat.

Beloved,
    How do you do that?
    How do you know exactly when to
        lighten me up with that
    fly-away laughter of yours –
        the kind that percolates
          right out of you?
    The kind that you've reserved
        just for me?
    Do you know how much that laughter
        means to me?
    What your delight does?
    Every time I hear it,
      another place swings open
        inside me.
    Thanks for not holding back.

Oh no!
>	I hadn't realized how spoiled I've become
>	by being with you so steadily.

Last night,
>	you asked me to follow you
>	to come right away.

That following was a hard thing,
>	because it meant taking
>	an immediate leave of another,
>	and doing what was right,
>	>	over what was polite.
>	And I chose polite!

I turned from you
>	and paid the price.

You stopped because you were through,
>	and so was the anointing.

You asked,
>	*Are you coming? It's time to go.*

But I was busy.

So you let me finish up by myself.

Beloved,
    I can't bear to be without you.
        What have I done?
        I am bereft
            over having stepped away
            from you yesterday,
            so saddened,
            that I can't quite hear you today.
        With remorse, I turn and confess all.
        It is not you who heaps me with shame.
        The moment I spoke it,
            it was over –
            forgiven and forgotten.
        You are ready to be with me now,
            dancing once again.
        Help me move
            onto the dance floor?

If any of you lacks wisdom,
he should ask God,
who gives generously to all
without finding fault,
and it will be
given to him.

James 1:5

Beloved?
    What did I think,
    That I would never step away from you?
    Never make a wrong choice
        or a mistake
    because I know how
        magnificent you are?
        I have overestimated my freedom.
    How ridiculous to think I can be you.
    Why should I be surprised
        by my human nature.
    I give up that wishful thinking now,
        and accept that I will fail.
    I accept my need of you.
    Thank you for a conscience -
        your sensitivity
    that says, "No good – don't go there."
    In a breath of repentance,
        we are restored to each other
    and I can look you full in the face again.

Beloved,
    I need to understand
        that you have
        forgiven me.
  I choose fact over feeling,
  otherwise,
        I will be going backward,
        eyes on the water,
        trying to get back into the boat,
    believing that
    somehow it's up to me
    to have no fault.
  I can't let the lie pull me under:
        "I will *work*
        so I can *earn*."
  It's the truth of your grace alone
        that saves me:
my Beloved has given me
        The Great Gift,
and now it is mine.
  I will not undermine my freedom.

This hair shirt

        is itchy

    and it's making me

    look down at the waves.

It's off, Beloved!

    It may be a strange gift,

        but it's yours.

(Phillip has just asked Jesus to *show us the Father*. Jesus tells him, *Anyone who has seen me has seen the Father…*)

The words I say to you are not just my own. Rather, it is the Father, living in me, who is doing his work…I tell the truth, anyone who has faith in me will do what I have been doing. He will do even greater things than these [miracles], because I am going to the Father. And I will do whatever you ask in my name, so that the Son may bring glory to the Father. You may ask me for anything in my name, and I will do it.

John 14: 10, 12-14

Beloved!
    I'm right here,
        right in front of you!
    Keep looking!
    Come on!
    You're almost there!
Nope, I won't let you go under,
    just hold on to me.
You're doing fine.
    I'm so proud of you!
    Keep walking!
Yup, we're still on top.
    Don't mind the waves,
    they'll cool you off.
I'm right in front of your eyes!
    You have beautiful eyes.
We're going to make it.

*If you remain in me
and my words remain in you,
ask whatever you wish,
and it will be given you.
This is to my Father's glory…
You did not choose me,
but I chose you and appointed you
to go and bear fruit –
fruit that will last.
Then the Father will give you
whatever you ask in my name.
This is my command:
love each other.*

John 15: 7-8, 16-17

You're very quiet today.
    I'm waiting to hear from you.
    What do you want to tell me?
    Tell me, Beloved,
        what is it?
    Okay then,
        what can I do for you today?
    Tell me what I need to know
        for my next step.

    Hello?
    Where are you?
        What's up?
    I'm listening…
    Why aren't you speaking?
    You always communicate to me.
        Why aren't you speaking?
    HELLO?
        Beloved…?…

        My, you're quiet today.

You're still quiet.

Beloved, I miss you.

I really am missing you.

Where are you?

If I don't hear your voice

    I may fade away.

You know that you're my life.

    You're my breath.

How can you be my Beloved

    and not speak to me,

    your very heart?

I don't do well without you,

    and just a reminder,

didn't you say,

    I will never leave you

    or forsake you ?

Okay, so if you haven't left,

then there is a reason for this hiatus.

I will wait,

    and do what I know to do.

I love you, my darling.

I've been thinking.
I just want you to know
    that I'm here
    and re-reading your
    love letters.
I remember what you last told me,
    and am seeing you
    overflowing with love
    and laughter and wisdom.
I love you so much,
    am so in love with you.
I do adore you when you're
on the move, or advising me.
Do I trust you during your quietness?
You have your reasons
    for everything you do.
Yes, I trust you entirely.
I read: *"In quietness and confidence shall be your strength."*
    (Isaiah 30:15 KJV)
Thank you for imparting your strength
    to me.

Beloved.

    Beloved…

beloved,

    beloved!

*Like an apple tree
among the trees of the forest
is my lover...
Strengthen me with raisins,
refresh me with apples, for I am
faint with love...
All night long on my bed
I looked for the one
my heart loves.*

Song of Songs 2: 3,5; 3:1

Beloved,
> I think I understand
> what you wanted me to know.

Before, you were a big part of my life;
> now you *are* my life.

I really do trust you –

I belong to you.

It is my desire to spend my life
> in worship –
> every minute, if it's possible.

It doesn't matter
> if I feel you as close or not.

Do you know why?

Because I know that you're in love with me.

And you can do whatever you want with me.

I will keep on doing all the things you love –
> things that show my trust and respect.

You are my own,

and I want to make you proud;

 I want people to see me and say,
> "There goes Beloved."

Was there ever such an adventure,
> as life with you, Beloved?

With you there is never a rut –
> you are a constant fresh breath –
> new idea, intoxicating thought,
> refreshing revelation.

There is enough pain and struggle
For us to appreciate it all.
Though your principles never change,
> the way you do things is always new.

You are the most fascinating soul ever!

With you there is never boredom!
> and yet, mystically, amazingly,

you blend the excitement with
> peace and opportunities to
> > practice patience and discipline!

You do this in a way that never ceases to
> stimulate me – there are endless hours

of delight with you, yet you are never
> too much.

You are just right.

You are plenty.

You are enough – but the kind that
> makes you want more of "enough" –
> a daily dose of delicious.

It's why I always want to be with you.

You have enchanted me utterly –
> spoiled me for all else, completely.

The books I used to read,
> the films I used to see,

what are they to me now?
> Claptrap, that's what –
> they are empty, flavorless and boring.

Once you've tasted a perfectly ripe peach,
> cotton candy is revealed for what it is:

no substitute for dinner –
> there's no nutrition there.

There'll be a sugar high,
> but you don't want to be around

when it wears off and you're semi-comatose.

With you, Beloved,
> I know that I am alive!

The same body that can experience deep pain,
> is the same one capable of great pleasure.

The ability to fear or love or trust,
> laugh or cry – sometimes both at once,

is a constant reminder that
> one who loves extravagantly

has made all this possible.

How resplendent this journey with you is!
It's a glory, not because it is easy,
> but because it is rich –

rife with highs and lows
> and everything in between.

As long as I can do it with you,
Beloved, I am satisfied –
> sated with the fullness of living.

You make me want to
> jump and shout –

I'm so glad that I can experience this.

You have made me *feel,* Beloved,
      And, through highs and lows,
this life will have been mine,
      and mine lavishly,
because of you.

Do you know how thankful I am?
I celebrate it all,
      because of your eyes
which have given me vision,
      and a new life
as beloved.
I love the mind that thought all this up.
Kisses to you, Beloved – forever!

I tell you the truth,
my Father will give you
whatever you ask
in my name.
Ask and you will receive
and your joy
will be complete.

John 16: 23-24

Sweetheart,
        Let's dance, can we?
There's nothing like being
        in your arms,
           twirling around the dance floor.
You have so many
        new steps to teach me.
        I want to learn them all.

Something came to me today,
> Beloved.
> When you are in a quiet, silent place,
> I must move on through the day
>> making my decisions
>> with the wisdom
>> I already have.
> You do not always need
>> to say something more.
> I have what I need.
> Most of the time I
>> "pray and obey."
> But if I can go to the right place
>> with what I've already learned,
> then I will simply
>> go.
> You have already supplied.

Today, Beloved,
>   There was too much din
>
>   from my body
>
>   for my mind to be able
>
>   to form the words to
>
>   talk with you
>
>   as we normally do.

No matter,
>   you came and simply
>
>   held me in your arms
>
>   as time became
>
>   timelessness.

How beautiful you are,
my darling!
Oh, how beautiful!

You are a garden fountain,
a well of flowing water...

Song of Songs 4: 1, 15

Beloved,
> Beloved.
> I need the rest that your spirit gives…
> Come,
>> take me away
>> into your intensive care.
> Hum through every cell,
>> gentling me with
>> whispers of love,
> too low for my ears to hear words,
> but of a calibration for my spirit
>> to catch every nuance.
> Take me away.
> and when I come out,
>> I'll be whole.

Beloved, This may be a tough one,
        but who else would I come to?
I am very, very angry …
I just now realize that I
        have never expressed anger to you…
But I am emotionally healed now,
        and feelings I once used to push down,
will no longer be muted and stored.
With you it is, not all or nothing,
        but all.
        So here goes.
        Do you want me to proceed?

        Come.

I am okay with my illness.
With you, I can handle it,
        but there's something I'm not okay with,
        and it's the suffering that
        I have to watch in
        someone I love deeply.

He has been in non-stop agony for
almost three months now,
and Beloved,
    I'm ANGRY,
And it feels like I AM ANGRY WITH YOU.
BELOVED, I'M SO ANGRY!

When I asked you to give me some
of what he was experiencing,
    you let me feel his despair.
So I go with despair and frustrated fury
      down to the basement now.
I'm gonna' hang this plastic bag
    full of old clothes over a beam.
I wrap my hands with pillow stuffing,
and light a cigar.
Yes, I am lighting this stupid cigar
    that says, "It's a boy."
It's the only thing I can control
    and I NEED TO PUFF!

I beat the tar out of this punching bag
    until I drop to the floor with it,
    spent,
    exhausted.
It's not you I'm pummeling, B,
    you know that, don't you?
But how long is this going to go on?
I have more questions for you:
    He's suffered for 50 years,
        what are you doing?
I thought it couldn't get much worse
    and it has.
Suffering to help bring people close to you,
    or to build character,
    or teach some lesson –
maybe there it makes sense,
    has a purpose.
But what purpose does this serve
when the afflicted one
    only seems to drop into desperation?

Is this how you treat the ones who love you?
Is this what you allow to happen to the ones
      you love?
You're no milquetoast lover,
      you're powerful and awesome.
If you are Beloved, and you are,
then act like him.
Why won't you find a way
      to break through, and either
      stop the agony
      or give some meaning to it
      so we can live around it?
I will not curse you.
I love you.
I love you so much, it hurts!
But I don't know what to do here.
      I can't help at all.
I know you experienced more pain than
      most of us will ever know
Your suffering was horrible,

(and God forgive me)
but you only had to endure it
> for a day,
>> not half a century.

Your hand is too heavy.
You ask too much,
> and sometimes I don't even know
> what you are asking.

What do we do?
I can deal with my own burden-
> with you it has felt do-able.

But this other burden,
> this other burden seems crushing.

I'm so tired, B, so tired.
Thanks for letting me vent.
Forgive me if I stepped over the line?
> Loving has worn me out.
> Help.

No eye has seen,
no ear has heard,
no mind has conceived
what God has prepared
for those who love him.
But God has revealed it
to us by his Spirit.
The Spirit searches all things,
even the deep things
of God.

I Corinthians 2: 9-12

After the anger a calm approaches.

Since I gave the gift of embarrassment

to Beloved several years ago

    for a New Year's present,

It's no longer here,

    so I leave my rantings with him

        and wait.

In an emotional limbo,

    I go to bed and sleep.

Maybe the rawness

    will develop a scab of numbness.

But in the morning

    I awake with something else:

    the quiet, familiar presence of Beloved,

    still here.

I don't see you hugging me,

    but just standing here,

    non-plussed,

    the same – rock solid.

I do detect a faint smile,

    yes, it is a faint smile

around the edges of your mouth.

It's not amusement.

    Is that pride I'm seeing?

Are you proud of me…?

    Good for you.

More!

You have been open and honest with me.
    Well done.
    This is what a healed one looks like.
Do you see how you are trusting me
    with your deepest feelings now?
    It's good to see you walking in truth.
    Now we can go somewhere new.

You didn't leave.

You didn't even flinch.

I've never minded a good wrestling match.

Apparently not.

Oh yeah – Jacob, Gideon, David …

Job.

> *So tell me,*
> *what knowledge did you*
> *wake with this morning?*

I know that apart from you I am nothing;
> I have nothing – no good thing.

I know that you are the only answer and
> the only thing that makes sense –
> even when you don't seem to.

I realize that miracles are happening, whether
> we're aware of them or not.

There is always benefit in what you allow.

What did I hear you tell me? You told me
> *This is not the end of the story.*

You want me to step aside…
> *…step out of the lasso*

You want me to step out of the lasso
> and wait.

You want me to stop trying, and be still.

You know that I will not stop talking to you
        about this, don't you?
Call me "Pitbull" if you want,
        but I will importune and thank you
        for the solution to this until I see it,
        don't you know?
        I do.
Then, Beloved,
        may I have this dance?

        It takes two to tango.

Beloved,
    There are times
        when your love
        shows its respect
        for my highest good,
not be an embrace,
but by a shared look
        from those intelligent,
        knowing eyes.
Instead of a caress,
        you give me
        what I need most right now:
the eyes of you as partner,
        burning into me
        the certainty of
        a higher understanding.
Smoldering,
        they hold me,
        transmitting the message:
You know the right thing to do. Do it.

I am my lover's
and my lover is mine.
This is my lover,
this my friend.

Song of Songs 6:3; 5:16

You grow me up,
> Beloved,
when instead of going heart to heart
we enjoin mind to mind,
> and you arrest me intellectually
> with a hint of your
> brilliant thoughts
> and genius plans.

We are partners,
> and the team
>> shouldn't be split up.

You give me the plain truth.
> I snap to.

Beloved,
    There are times –
    you know the ones,
that I purpose to
    not eat for awhile
    so that I can really
    listen to you,
    talk it out, or
    think and wait,
    letting worship lead the way.
Then there are times,
    like this morning,
    when the thought of food
takes flight to those faraway mountains.
Here I stand,
    rendered mute
    by the look of love on your face.

Beloved,
    You woke me
    at dawn
        with your whispers
  of love.
    Your need of me
        called out
        across the morning.
  I hurried from my bed
        to be with you.
  Will there ever be
        enough of you?
  I only ever want more.

Oh my lover,
> You came and got me,
> and your fire
>> burned healing in me,
>> setting all
>> surrounding kindlings
>> ablaze!

*Now to him who is able
to do immeasurably more
than all we ask
or imagine,
according to his power
that is at work within us,
to him be glory
in the church
and in Christ Jesus
throughout all generations,
for ever and ever!
Amen!*

Ephesians 3:20

Beloved,
    Pour out.
        Pour out…
        in your compassion,
        in your peace,
        in your holiness
        in your power.
    Drench me in the myrrh
        of eagerness
        to do your bidding.
        Pour out.
    Pour out.

Beloved,
    Only eternity
    will afford me
    the time
        I need with you.
    For now,
        I will love you,
        often and well,
        and as much as we are able.

Beloved,
        It is your voice
        I hear.
You,
        who sets my feet
        to dancing.
When you ask,
        "May I…?"
the yes shines on my face
        and you lead me
        to the dance floor.

My lover spoke and said to me,
Arise, my darling,
my beautiful one,
and come with me.
See!
The winter is past;
the rains are over and gone.
Flowers appear
on the earth;
the season of singing
has come,
the cooing of doves
is heard in our land.

Song of Songs 2: 10-13

Beloved,
> When I deserve you the least -
>> that's when I experience
>> your greatest generosity.

What?
> "There is never a moment
> when anyone deserves anything."

I see:
> Your great generosity is there
> all the time.

That is the truth
>> about earning – no one can.

And that is nature of
>> steadfast love – it's free.
>> Teach me.

Beloved,
> I treasure our
> lover's conversations.

I hope you feel the same.
I want to be the exhale
> of your inhale,
> breathed out by you

to make a difference in this world.
It is a pleasure
> to be sent on a mission
> by you.

Last week, when you directed me
> to approach the woman
> in the grocery store
> and ask her about her pain,

then pray with her,
she was astonished.
> "How did you know?" she asked.

"I don't know anything, but there's Someone
who knows everything about you
> and loves you."

She cried
> and listened.

People are captivated
> by your voice,
> by you,

Beloved.
They recognize truth
> when they hear it.

Or see it.
Let me be your arms
> to a hurting populace.

They can have you
> in my arms.

I'll tell them about
> my Beloved.
> Whisper love to me.

Keep whispering.

Beloved,
    Here's something else
    I love about you:
together,
    we can kick up our heels
    in non-apologetic excitement
and skip around in delight
    celebrating you
    and all the obvious good things
    that you do,
and just have a ball.
But then, in the next minute,
    when something has
come along and
    taken me down a notch,
the dance music
    keeps playing in the background
    even though the room
    has gotten quiet.

Beloved,
    This is a really tall mountain!
    My body harness is secure.
Yes,
    my helmet is strapped on
    goggles in place,
    plenty of running room,
Am I ready to jump?
Wait…
    just another minute,
    let me test these wings again.
Looks like a good windy day.
Ready if you are!
On three…
!!!!!!!

(We are to be)

encouraged in heart,
and united in love, so that
[we] may have the full riches
of complete understanding,
in order that [we] may know
the mystery of God,
namely, Christ,
in whom are hidden
all the treasures of
wisdom and knowledge.

Colossians 2: 2-3

Beloved,

About this question of spiritual ecstasy...

Someone actually told me that
    life is better lived
    on the emotionally straight road;
that highs and lows are too wearing,
    not necessary;
    and should be avoided.
I wanted to be annoyed,
    but thought I'd wait
    and talk to you about it first.
Oh, you make me laugh so often!
    You are reminding me of the
    "render unto Caesar" remark,
    only with your inimitable spin on it:
"The steady should render unto steadiness
    that which belongs to steady,
and the adventurers to adventuring,
    but both unto God."

Beloved,
    Wherever I go
   you are there.
      Out under the rain
         I am anointed by you;
     beneath a strong sun,
        you are my shade.
    The valleys
       cannot isolate me,
    the width of an ocean
       cannot cool your ardor,
    the hail storm or hurricane
       cannot mute the sound
       of your voice.
We are implored by love
    to seek the high places;
the high places of an unquiet love.

Beloved,
        The essence
        of my music
            is you.
        The melody is a glory
            to be heard.
        We go higher,
            and as we do,
            the mellifluence
        mirrors the release
            of a pure
            and
            exquisite
            pleasure.

Beloved,
    I sing,
        and my song is of you.
When I make music
    the melody,
    keys,
    chords
    and overtones,
underscore the praises
    of my Beloved.
My heart radiates,
    as my face
tells the story of one
    in love.

*I am my lover's
and my lover is mine...*

*How beautiful you are
and how pleasing,
O love,
with all your delights!*

I belong to my lover...

Song of Songs 6:3; 7:6,10

beloved,

    I yearn for you

        to come to me,

and you are here.

I drink of you,

    and my soul,

        my sum and substance

bathes

in refreshment.

Do you know

    what it means to me

    when you want to be with me?

Beloved,
    How
        can such love
            be?

Beloved,
> You played,
> as I sang,
> and the song
>> that broke forth
>> was new,
> one that I had never sung
>> before.
> It was the song of gladness –
>> of mourning
>> being dashed
>> in the presence of
Joy.

Beloved,
>Here is another worship gift for you:
>Today someone lit into me
>>with a tirade of rage.
>People will say anything, won't they?
>>I guess you know all about that!
>There was no reason this man should
>>be angry with me,
>the guy was just having a bad day,
>>but I could see he was gonna' blow.
>He did. And he kept right on blowing.
>You gave me grace to answer kindly,
>>but I could see he was ready
>>to unleash round two.,
>so I excused myself and went out to pray:
>>"Help him and give me patience."
>You bolstered me up and sent me back in.
>He was still there, having his bad day.
>I nodded and prayed silently for him again
>>before I left.

*Dear friends,
If our hearts do not condemn us,
we have confidence before God,
and receive from him
anything we ask,
because we obey his commands
and do what pleases him.*

I John 3:22

Beloved,
> Though the war has been won,
> I know that there is a battle raging,
> with every beloved in the epicenter.

I stand with you in dealing with
> the "spiritual wickedness
>> in high places,"
> and the accuser

who wants to destroy our relationship.

In Jesus' name
> I bind all who would raise up
> against the name of Jesus,

and command that they be bound and sent
> to the feet of the one true
> Lord Jesus Christ
> to be dealt with.

No one messes with us
> and gets away with it.

I am my Beloved's
> and he is mine.

Beloved,

Something's come up

    and I am unsure of what to do,

        where to go.

Usually, when this happens -

  if I don't have clear direction

    or certain bearings,

      I do nothing.

      I wait.

You've shown me the wisdom

of giving something new

    the breathing space

        of a little time.

          There is only one thing

      of importance here,

and this I do know:

I am in your hands, my Darling

and I will not be moved

      until you, Beloved

        move me.

Beloved,
      I'm moving!
        You have spoken,
   given discernment,
      added revelation –
spoken clearly.

     Let's go!

We're making tracks
   in your time now,
and nothing can
      hold us back!

Beloved,

You are

> The Perfect One,
>
> Spotless Lamb,
>
> Rose of Sharon,
>
> Lion of Judah,
>
> Banner of Love,
>
> One Who Gave Himself For Me,
>
> My Delight,
>
> My Darling,
>
> Alpha,
>
> Omega,
>
> Everything In-Between,
>
> The Kisses of My Mouth,
>
> My Heart,
>
> My Lover,
>
> My Passion,
>
> My Purest Beloved.

beloved,

> *You are my*
>> *Fellowship,*
>> *Fulfilled longing,*
>> *Arms,*
>> *Heart,*
>> *Temple,*
>> *Joy,*
>> *Beauty,*
>> *Channel of blessing,*
>> *Compassion to the world,*
>> *Bride,*
>> *Family,*
>> *Reason for loving,*
>> *Strong one,*
>> *Fruitful delight,*
>> *My passion,*
>> *My pure beloved.*

Place me like a seal
over your heart,
like a seal on your arm;
for love is as strong
as death,
it's jealousy unyielding
as the grave.
It burns like blazing fire,
like a mighty flame.
Many waters cannot wash it away.

Song of Songs 8: 6,7

Beloved!

*For God so loved the world that he gave
his one and only Son,
that whoever believes in him
shall not perish but
have eternal life.*

John 3:16

Beloved!

*The Lord your God
is with you,
he is mighty to save.
He will take great delight
in you,
he will quiet you
with his love,
He will rejoice over you
with singing.*

Zephaniah 3:17

Beloved, master of the high adventure,
>	you never stop astonishing
>	>	and delighting me;
>	Every time I come to you,
>	>	you answer me in a new
>	>	and effective way.
I've always known
>	how perfect,
>	how majestic
>	and creative you are,
but now that I'm experiencing
>	the Beloved who is
>	practical
while being efficient, fun
>	and funny…!
Well, who knew there were
>	all these sides to you?
Before my healing,
>	even right after the big one,

there were old habits to be shed.
    I was not yet turning down all my
        temptations,
and was still dealing with
    some addictions.
There were certain behaviors
and responses that needed to go.
But as I began to walk out
    my healing
    and live in the new ways,
the old became discomfiting,
but weren't yet distasteful enough
    to scrap.
 I didn't know how to change these.
    But maybe, more truthfully,
I was unwilling to leave such
    comfortable old buddies behind.
"Beloved show me specifically how
to do this" I asked you, remember?

"Help me to want you more than my old ways.
Please, give me what it takes to turn away
>   from wanting anything
>   that would hurt you or me."

And that's when you dropped into my mind,
>   three things to do:

First, you had me ask myself,
>   Where did the desire for this thing
>   >   originate?

Whoosh! I was back in the memory
>   and feeling the same things
>   >   I feel before this addiction kicks in now.

There in the child, sat anger.
>   and beneath the anger sat frustration.

And at the bottom of both were the real culprits
>   - powerlessness and invalidation.

I asked you to address those.
>   and Beloved, you did.

You came into the memory with me,
>   but didn't look at it, only at me.

Then you took me by the hand and led me
> cheerfully away from it.

You snorted in derision,

What have these things to do with you?

And that did it.

Their power was gone.

The lies I had believed, were replaced
> by the look on your face
> which effectively told me:

You are filled with all power –
> *Mine! And it is yours.*

You are loved, cared for and important.

And this truth went into the core of me.

The lies were smashed
> like the cockroaches they were.
> And I walked away with you.

The flow of forgiveness was enough
> to cover everyone in the scene.

Then the scene faded away into nothingness.

And here's where it gets even better:

It was time for the third piece
      of your direction.
The next time that temptation came knocking,
      I was ready for it.
I could almost hear it say, in its silky way,
      "I'm h-e-e-e-re."
It was simple – I called your name
and gestured you forward, Beloved,
      then stepped behind you.
You moved in front of me,
      folded your arms
      and confronted the accuser:
Did you call for me?
you said in that Jehovah voice of yours.
I got to watch temptation
      shrivel and fade away,
      right in front of my eyes.
I felt like Dorothy in Oz,
      with a ringside seat,
      watching the wicked witch
            melt.

You are so cool.

I've never felt safer,
> more protected
> or stronger.

This is power!

Really, I cannot get over
> the many facets to you.

You're ready to step up to the plate
> on my behalf in a heartbeat.

You just need to be asked.

I know I'll need to ask you
> every time.

But I can, because I know your voice,
> and know that I can trust it.

I trust you, Beloved.

And because of that,
> new worlds are opening
> every day.

I cannot wait for more adventures with you!

Song of Songs 6:3

*I am my lover's
and my lover is mine.
NIV*

*I am my beloved's,
and my beloved is mine.
KJV*

INDEX

9	Introduction
17	A prayer to become his child
18	A prayer of intent (dedication)
19	Song of Songs 2:10-13
20	"I'm head over heels…"
21	"All these years I've wanted you…"
22	"I am to squander your love here…"
23	"If we become what we love…"
24	"You are my intoxicant, the exhilaration of living…"
25	Joshua 1:5
26	"Love compels me toward a simpatico with you…"
27	"I dream about you, you know…"
28	"One of your most endearing qualities"
29	"'How do I love thee'…?" (astound him with my faith…)
31	Isaiah 30:19-21
32	"it is all gone…i'm shivering…"
33	"I cannot think, but I know…"
34	"you…unmoored me from my sadness"
35	Psalm 3:4; 10:17-18
36	"Break me open and let the scent of spices…"
37	Psalm 16:7; 17:6-7

38	"swan diving into the pool…"
39	"when I ebb, you flow…"
40	"How do you …sear the wounds…?"
41	Psalm 26:7; 25:14
42	"Dearest…you have healed me…"
43	"Let's sing!"
44	"Beloved, I am lovesick…"
45	"love will not be stilled…"
46	"Was there ever such an adventure…?"
47	Song of Songs 1:2
48	"I am heavy lidded with love…"
49	"the place where my mind resides…"
50	"A release can only occur…"
51	"Set my tempo today…"
52	John 10:27
53	"You have emancipated me…"
54	"Darling, let me sky-write your name…"
55	"I've become a pulsar…"
56	Song of Songs 1:15
57	"Let's have breakfast out on the porch.."
58	"Do you know how much your laughter means?"
59	"I turned from you…"
60	"I can't bear to be without you…"
61	James 1:5
62	"Did I think I would never step away?"
63	"You have forgiven me…"
64	"This hair shirt is itchy…"
65	John 14: 10,12-14
66	*"I won't let you go under…"*

67	John 15:7-8
68	"You're very quiet today…"
69	"You're still quiet…I'm missing you…"
70	"Do I trust you during your quietness?"
71	Beloved. Beloved… *beloved...*
72	Song of Songs 2:3,4; 3:1
73	"..see me and say, 'There goes Beloved"
74	"Was there ever such an adventure…?"
78	John 16:23-24
79	"Let's dance, can we?"
80	"When you are …quiet… I will simply go."
81	"…hold me in your arms until time becomes timelessness."
82	Song of Songs 4:15
83	"Come take me away into your intensive care."
84	"I'm so angry! (When God says 'No.)
89	I Corinthians 2:9-12
90	"After the anger, a calm approaches."
94	"The eyes of you as partner, burn into me."
95	Song of Songs 6:3; 5:16
96	"…you give me the plain truth…"
97	"…rendered mute by the look of love…"
98	"You woke me at dawn with your whispers of love…"
99	"Oh my lover, you came and got me…"
100	Ephesians 3:20
101	"drench me in the myrrh of eagerness to do your bidding."

102	"Only eternity will afford me the time I need with you."
103	"It is…you who sets me feet to dancing."
104	Song of Songs 2:10-13
105	"When I deserve you the least…"
106	"I treasure our lover's conversations…"
108	"We can kick up our heels…"
109	"Looks like a good, windy day…"
110	Colossians 1:9
111	"About the question of spiritual ecstasy…"
112	"…seek the high places of an unquiet love."
113	"…a pure and exquisite pleasure…"
114	"I sing, and my song is of you."
115	Song of Songs 6:3; 7:6,10
116	*"I yearn for you to come to me…"*
117	"…how can such love be?"
118	"…the song of gladness – of mourning being dashed…"
119	"…the guy was just having a bad day."
120	I John 3:22
121	"There is a battle raging…"
122	"I will not be moved, until you move me."
123	"…nothing can hold us back!"
124	"You are my… Purest Beloved."
125	*"You are my pure beloved."*
126	Song of Songs 8:6,7

127   John 3:16
128   Zephaniah 3:17
129   "Beloved, master of the high adventure!"

(The Apostle Paul speaking to believers)

I keep asking
that the God of our Lord Jesus Christ,
the glorious Father,
may give you
the Spirit of wisdom and revelation,
so that you may know him better.

Ephesians 1:17

Poems by Topic

Adventure: 38,46,55,57,74,79,94,98,103, 108,109,129

Anger: 84-88

Comfort: 21,33,34,39,49,50,57,66,81,83, 94,105,112,121,123

Confidence/Assurance: 23,24,26,33,39,46, 50,53,99,121,123,125

Desperation: 32,33,34,84-88

Faith/Faithfulness: 22,29-30,33,34,39,40, 42,60,68,73,80,81,83,9093,99,101,105, 112,118,121,122,123,129-134

Forgiveness: 29-30,59,60,63

Fasting: 97

Freedom: 23,24,36,38,41,42,43,46,50,53, 54.55.63.64.74,77.79.98.99.103.108. 109,111,112,118,123,129-134

Fun: 28,43,46,54,57,58,74-77,79,103,108, 109,111,129-134

God's Laughter: 28,58

God's Longings: 29-30,39,44,45,46,50, 51,55,57,74,75-77,79,81,83,90-93,96 98,99,112,116,125

Grace: 38,39,59-63,195,117,129-134

Grief: 32-34.40-43,53,81,83,90-93,99

Healing, process of healing: 32-34,40-43,53,81,83,90-93,99,118

Loving Others/Ministry: 22,45,54,73, 84-88,106-107,119

Passionate Love Scriptures:

19,104	Song of Songs 2:10-13
47	Song of Songs 1:2
56	Song of Songs 1;5
72	Song of Songs 2:3,5; 3:1
82	Song of Songs 4:1, 15
95	Song of Songs 6:3; 5:16
115	Song of Songs 6:3; 7:6, 10
127	John 3:16

Peace: 33,34,40,51,57,63,81,90,113

Perseverance, patience: 21,68-71,80,84-8 88,102,121,122,123,129-134

Release: 34,38,42,43,50,53,54,64,84-88,90, 103.109.111.113,118.121.123.129-134

Repentance: 60,62,84,88

Salvation: 17,54,63,105,127

Scriptures on Two-way Prayer:
(God answering us)

25	Joshua 1:5
31	Isaiah 30: 19-21
35	Psalm 3:4; 10: 17-18
37	Psalm 16:7; 17: 6-7
41	Psalm 26:7; 25:14
52	John 10:27
61	James 1:5
67	John 15:7,8; 16:7
78	John 16: 23-24
100	Ephesians 3:20
110	Colossians 1:9
120	I John 3:22
142	Ephesians 1:17

Spiritual Ecstasy: 12,19,20,23,24,26,38, 43,44,46,47,48,54,56,71,79,95,98,99, 102,103,104,106,108,111,113,114, 116,117,124,125

Spiritual Growth:
20,21,22,23,38,40,42,46,55,70,73,84-88, 94,101,106-107,111,119,121,129-134

Spiritual Warfare 40,42,46,99,121,129-134

Suffering: 32-33 (to54).36,40, 42,66,70,71, 81,84-88,90-93,121

Thankfulness: 21,26,29-30,38,40,44,53,55, 75-77,90-93,97,99,101,114,118,129-134

Worship: 23,24,43,71,79,81,97,98,102,106-107, 113,114,119,124

Roadblocks to hearing from God:

- Not being his (Matthew 13: 11-15)

- Unconfessed sin (Psalm 66:18)

- Unforgiveness (Mt.6: 12, 14-15)

- Emotional & spiritual baggage from wounds of the past.(Examples of people in Scripture before and after healings shows the change in how they respond to God.) Emotional pain distorts truth and sidetracks the person from knowing God and hearing him, because of lies that are believed. It is the accuser's intention to pervert truth, discredit God and shut down the believer. God's plan is to address the core lies behind our wounds and heal them so we can be free.